Science Experiments for the Primary Grades

By ROBERT W. REID

Professor of Elementary Education

Eastern Washington State College

Fearon Teacher Aids
a division of
David S. Lake Publishers
Belmont, California

ISBN-0-8224-6300-8

Printed in the United States of America.

CONTENTS

INTRODUCTION

The experiments given in this book were developed by the author and used in an in-service program with primary grades teachers. The teachers were furnished with a large number of experiments, which they tried with their classes. The teachers were then asked to rate the experiments on a five-point scale in the following areas: value to all of the children in the class, value to only some of the children in the class, interest to children, understanding by children, and teacher's ability to perform experiments. The experiments selected for this book were those rated highest by the teachers.

The experiments can be conducted with a minimum of equipment. Most of them are simple enough to be performed by the children themselves, but they are just as effective in introducing and emphasizing many scientific principles and concepts as are more complex experiments. In fact, when an experiment is kept as simple as possible, the attention of the children tends to focus to a greater degree upon the experiment rather than the apparatus.

Because many of the concepts introduced are basic ones, it is possible for the explanations and discussions to become involved. Too little discussion will not satisfy the healthy curiosity of children and too much or too deep an explanation might be wasted or, even worse, tend to confuse the children. The explanations in this book were purposely kept as brief as possible, for the nature of the experiments themselves tends to provide readily apparent explanations in most cases.

Not all the experiments in a particular area will be needed to teach the various concepts to all children. Some children will need a variety of different experiences before they have gained even a partial understanding of the principles involved. Other children, perhaps with richer backgrounds of experience, would be bored by many repetitions; they should be encouraged to move deeper into the areas of science they have begun to explore. Teachers may hesitate to repeat experiments for fear that they will not be fresh to the children. It should be remembered that the same principles of learning that apply in other areas, repetition and spaced review, apply to learning through experiments. Evaluation must be made continually to determine whether experiments have been successful in helping the child to learn basic science concepts.

The experiments given in this book will, no doubt, suggest other possibilities to the teacher. Care must be exercised, however, to limit the variables as much as possible. In other words, when experimental comparison is made, all things should be as nearly alike as possible, with one exception. For instance, two similar plants in similar containers may be used to observe what happens when a plant does not receive light. One plant is covered by a paper bag and the other left uncovered. The teacher is indeed fortunate if the children ask some critical questions. Is any light going through the bag? Do both plants receive the same amount of water? Is more moisture evaporating from one plant than the other? Are both plants receiving the same amount of "air"? It is neither practical nor necessary for the teacher to attempt to limit all but one of the possible variables every time, but she should attempt to make the comparison as scientific as possible.

Children, too, should be made aware of the possibilities. It might be said that perhaps the most important learning comes not from what the experiment shows, but from a discussion of the experiment itself and the controls used. The teacher should use the experiments not only to help children develop concepts, but also to aid them in building attitudes, such as using evidence to reach a conclusion, using caution about making "absolute" statements and drawing inferences, and looking for reasons for behavior and events. The teacher should help children to understand that none of these experiments, by itself, really proves anything, but that all of the experiments indicate possibilities and even probabilities in connection with cause and effect.

ROBERT W. REID

Chapter One

PLANTS

1. PLANT GROWTH

(a) Light

Material: potted plant

Place a potted plant on a window sill. Note that it leans toward the light. Turn the plant a half circle and observe any changes.

(b) Heat and cold

Materials: two similar potted plants

Place one plant outdoors and one in a heated room during the winter. Compare the two plants, observing the effects of winter climate in temperate zones.

(c) Water

Materials: two pots of fertile soil, several bean seeds, and water

Plant several untreated bean seeds at equal depths in each of the two pots. Place the pots in a warm, light place. Water one pot regularly and leave the other dry. Observe the results.

PLANTING GUIDE

Plant	Average Planting Depth of Seeds	Approximate Time to Grow to Maturity
Beans, green	¾″	65 days
Beans, Lima	¾″	90 days
Beans, snap	¾″	60 days
Beets	¼″	60 days
Carrots	¼″	70 days
Corn	1½″	75-90 days
Cucumbers	1¼″	70 days
Lettuce	¼″	60 days
Peas	1¼″	60 days
Pumpkins	1″	100 days
Radishes	½″	30 days
Watermelons	1″	80 days

(d) Buds

Materials: branches with buds and a container of water

Place budding branches of pussy willow, apple, or pear in a container of water and watch the swelling and opening of the buds.

2. PLANT SPROUTING

(a) Potatoes and carrots

Materials: potatoes, carrots, and a container of water

Place potatoes and carrots in water and observe the subsequent sprouting.

(b) Beans

Materials: shallow pan, pan cover, paper towels, six bean seeds, and water

Fit a paper towel in a shallow pan. Moisten the towel with water. Place the bean seeds evenly on the towel and cover them with another moistened towel. Place the cover over all but a small area of the pan. (The cover helps keep the moisture from evaporating rapidly; a small uncovered area will provide some ventilation.) Then put the pan in a shady location. Keep the towels moist. The seeds should sprout in a few days. Seeds may also be sprouted in moist moss or sand.

(c) Sprouting time

Materials: various kinds of seeds, a container of fertile
        soil, and water

Plant different kinds of seeds at the same depth. Select
an average depth from the various recommended plant-
ing depths for the seeds used. Provide water, light, and
warmth and note how long each kind of seed takes to
sprout. Sprouting time may be graphed, charted, or placed
on a calendar.

3. PLANTING DEPTH

Materials: various kinds of seeds, a large glass container
        of soil (an aquarium, for example), and water

Place 1" of soil in the container. Place various seeds on the
soil next to the glass. Add more soil and seeds in the same
manner until the container is full. Provide water, warmth,
and light and observe which seeds grow best at each level.
A labelled chart of the various seeds planted will help children to identify the growing seeds. Arrow-shaped labels of
masking tape may be attached to the glass to point to
certain seeds.

4. PLANT ROOTS

Materials: ivy slip and a container of water

Bring an ivy slip to school. Place it in water and observe
root formation and growth.

5. PLANT ROOTS AND SHOOTS

Materials: several large seeds; two equal-sized plates of
        glass 6" to 10" square; string; a blotter; a brick
        or rock; a shallow cake pan, bread pan, or
        cookie sheet; and water

The blotter should be trimmed to the size of the glass plates
used. Wet the blotter thoroughly and lay it on one glass
plate. Arrange some large seeds on the blotter at least 2"
from any edge of the blotter. Place the other piece of glass
on top. Tie the three layers together securely with string
and place the "sandwich" on edge in a pan containing
about ½" of water. A brick or rock placed in the pan pro-
vides convenient support for the upright "sandwich." Refill
the pan regularly with water to the ½" level to keep the

9

lower edge of the blotter wet. Observe the sprouting of the seeds and note the shoots going up and the roots going down. Turn the plates one-quarter turn so that they rest on one of the former vertical edges yet remain upright. Observe what happens to the now-horizontal roots and shoots. Do they remain horizontal? Do they all live? The glass may be marked and root and shoot growth measured and charted for various seeds.

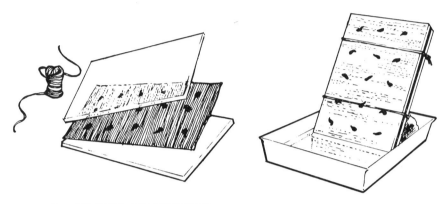

6. PLANT CROWDING

Materials: about a dozen seeds and a container of fertile soil at least 12″ in length

Plant six seeds at the same depth and no more than ¼″ apart. Plant another group of the same kind of seeds at the same depth as the first group, but space them 4″ to 6″ apart. Observe which group of plants seems to grow better.

7. PLANT SEEDS

(a) Embryos

Materials: Lima bean or butter bean seeds and a container of water

Soak the seeds in water overnight. Open the seeds to see the embryos (future baby plants) inside the seeds.

(b) Seeds contain air

Materials: About 20 bean seeds, a small water glass, and warm water

Place the bean seeds in the glass and fill it with enough warm water to cover the seeds. Note the small bubbles of air that escape. Remove the seeds and examine them to find the tiny hole that allows water to be admitted for germination.

(c) Other uses

Materials: a container of fertile soil, several seed peanuts, a piece of tablet paper, a pan, and an oven

Plant seed peanuts and provide the water, warmth, and sunlight necessary for growth. Why is the peanut sometimes called "the seed that buries itself"? Roast some of the raw peanuts on a pan in the oven. Compare the taste of the roasted peanuts with the raw peanuts. Make peanut butter by crushing some of the roasted peanuts on a piece of tablet paper. Observe the fats and oils that make peanut butter sticky.

Chapter Two

EARTH

1. ROCKS

(a) Wearing

Materials: two rocks, several inches in size, of a relatively soft material such as sandstone

Rub two rocks together to show how friction may wear down rocks. Observe how much rock wears away. Discuss how much wearing must take place, and for how long, to cause rocks to become smooth. Discuss wearing of hard and soft rocks to make hills, ridges, and mountains.

(b) Weight (erosion)

Materials: sand, pebbles, a large spoon, and a jar of water

Stir some sand and pebbles into the jar of water. Notice how the pebbles and the sand drop to the bottom of the

jar as the water slows and stops moving. Discuss the erosion of soil by water.

(c) Breaking

Materials: a pint or quart jar with a screw cap, a bucket or pan, water, and porous rock

To show how water can break things through expansion when it freezes, fill a jar with water and screw a jar lid on tightly. Place the jar in an empty bucket or pan (to avoid later handling of broken glass and the spreading of water from melting ice). If the outside temperature is below freezing, place the bucket containing the jar outdoors until the water freezes and the jar breaks. If the outside temperature is above about 25° F., the bucket with the jar may be placed in a food freezer for a short period to obtain similar results. Discuss how rocks can be broken by water and cold. Examine porous rocks to find how water can enter the rock.

2. SOIL

(a) Air

Materials: a pint or quart glass jar, soil, and water

Fill the jar about half full of soil. Add water until the jar is almost full and note the air bubbles that escape. Observe that soil contains air.

(b) Water

Materials: a one-gallon can, an electric hot plate, a sheet of glass large enough to cover the open top of the can, and garden soil

Fill the can about half full of garden soil and heat it gently on the electric hot plate. Note the beads of moisture that form on the inside of the top half of the can. Cover the can with the piece of glass and observe the moisture that appears on the glass. To show that all of the moisture does not come from the air inside the can, repeat the experiment without placing any soil in the can and compare the results.

3. SOIL BRICKS

Materials: ground clay, straw, a scrap board, a pan or a bucket, and water

Mix some clay, straw, and water in a pan or bucket. Add only enough water to the clay and straw to make a doughy mixture. Mold the mixture into bricks and place the bricks on a board. Dry the bricks in the sun. If the weather is too damp for drying outside, the bricks may be dried in an oven. Discuss how heat may harden dirt into rock or hard substances such as pottery and china dishes.

4. SOIL MOVEMENT

(a) Water

Materials: a quart glass jar with a screw lid, soil, and water

Fill the jar about one-quarter full of loose, fine soil, and fill the remainder of the jar with water. Cover the jar and shake it rapidly until the soil and water are thoroughly mixed. Observe that water can "hold" soil. Discuss how

13

soil might be carried by water. Take the mixture outdoors and pour it out on the ground. Does the soil travel with the water? Mix a second jar of soil and water and allow the soil to settle to the bottom of the jar. Discuss what happens when water in rivers or streams that are carrying soil slows down or stops moving. If a bank of loose soil is available near the school, this concept may be further illustrated by pouring water down the bank. Erosion by water may also be demonstrated by building a small "hill" of dirt on an otherwise empty sand table and following the same procedure.

(b) Wind

Materials: an electric fan, a sheet of paper about 3' square, and a small quantity of dust

Direct the draft of an electric fan on a small pile of dry, fine soil (dust) on a sheet of paper to demonstrate how wind can move soil. Show how dunes are formed.

Chapter Three

WATER

1. WATER AND FLOATING

(a) *Materials:* a large glass jar or aquarium filled with water, and various small objects — an eraser, a paper clip, a pencil, a block of wood, etc.

Try floating various objects in the water in the container. Observe which objects float and which ones sink.

(b) *Materials:* an empty coffee can, a pan 10" or 12" in size, a larger pan (dish pan, for example), about a dozen pebbles, a small block of wood, and water

Place the small pan inside the larger pan. Fill the small pan with water until it is completely full. (It may be filled until it overflows to be sure it is full.) Carefully place and float the block of wood in the water. Observe that some water flows out of the inner pan and that floating objects take up space in water. Refill the inner pan and float an empty coffee can in the water. Place pebbles in the coffee can. What happens to the water? Compare the can to an empty boat and a loaded boat.

(c) *Materials:* several 2″ squares of lead foil, a large jar or aquarium filled with water, and paper clips

Bend one 2″ square of lead foil into the form of a boat and place it on the surface of the water in the container. It will float because the weight of the water it displaces is equal to or greater than its own weight. If an object is heavier than the weight of the water it displaces, it will sink. This may be demonstrated by placing paper clips in the toy boat until the water comes in over the top and the boat sinks. Show that a similar 2″ square of lead foil will sink in water if it is left flat or balled. Try "boats" of different sizes and shapes.

2. EVAPORATION

(a) Water

Materials: two similar pieces of cloth 8″ square or larger, a piece of wax paper or foil larger than the two pieces of cloth, and water

Wet the two pieces of cloth and place them on the wax paper or foil. Roll one piece into a ball and spread the other one flat on the wax paper or foil. Which piece dries first? Why?

(b) Rain

Materials: a saucer, a large glass jar or aquarium, a sheet of glass large enough to cover the top of the jar or aquarium, and water

Fill the saucer with water and place it on the bottom of the jar. Cover the jar with the glass. The next day, note that moisture has condensed on the cover. Tap the cover to simulate rain. The saucer of water may be likened to the ocean and the other bottom area of the jar to land. Such a comparison may be used to show that it may rain on both land and ocean. Discuss snow. Ask what controls might be used to make this experiment more scientific. (Repeat the experiment as before but do not fill the saucer with water.)

3. STEAM

Materials: a teakettle with water, an electric hot plate, and a mirror or a piece of glass at least 6″ square

Boil water in the teakettle to make steam. Note the condensation above the spout of the kettle. Observe that the steam is visible when condensation starts. Hold the mirror or piece of glass near the spout. Observe the surface of the glass. What happens? Care must be exercised with this experiment because steam can scald! Why does a singing teakettle "sing"?

4. WATER – GRAVITY AND PRESSURE

Materials: a piece of glass tubing 6″ to 8″ long, a piece of rubber tubing about 12″ long, a funnel, a pail, and water

The diameter of the glass tubing and the diameter of the small end of the funnel should be about the same. The rubber tubing should have a diameter just large enough to permit it to slip tightly over the ends of the glass tubing and the funnel. Connect the short piece of glass tubing and the funnel by means of the rubber tubing. Hold this apparatus in the shape of a "U." Have an assistant fill the apparatus with water until the funnel is about half full. Observe that the water in the glass tube stays as high as the water in the funnel. Place your finger over the open end of the glass tube and hold the funnel higher than the

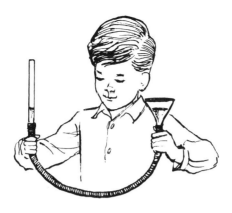

glass tube. Remove your finger from the end of the glass tube and let the water gush into the pail. Note that water seeks its own level. Vary the repetition of the experiment by raising the funnel in small steps and comparing the levels at each step. Discuss water and hills, city water lines, and kitchen faucets.

5. WATER — FILTERING

Materials: a glass jar, dirt, pebbles, a bucket, a wire kitchen strainer, either a piece of filter paper or a section of a nylon stocking, and water

Mix some dirt and pebbles with water in the glass jar. Pour the mixture through the wire strainer into the bucket. Refill the jar from the mixture in the bucket. Repeat the process using filter paper or a piece of nylon stocking. Observe the filters. Is water that looks clean always pure?

6. ICE

(a) *Materials:* an empty milk carton, a shallow pan, a weather thermometer, water, and access to a food freezer or the freezing compartment of a refrigerator if the outside temperature is above freezing

Use the thermometer to determine if the outside temperature is below freezing. Place the thermometer in the freezer or freezing compartment of the refrigerator and compare the temperature there with the outside temperature. Fill the milk carton about half full of water. Place it outside if the temperature is below freezing, or in the freezer or freezing compartment. Allow time for the water to freeze. Bring the carton of ice into the room and place it in the shallow pan. Tear off the paper carton and watch the ice melt. Discuss frozen rivers and lakes. What happens when the weather gets warm?

(b) *Materials:* a food freezer or a refrigerator with a freezing compartment if the outside temperature is above freezing, a milk carton or an ice cube tray, and a large pan of water

Fill the milk carton or the ice cube tray half full of water and freeze the water. Fill the large pan about half full of water. Remove the ice from the container and place it in the pan of water. Note that the ice floats. Discuss the fact that when water freezes it expands and increases in volume, and the ice is, therefore, lighter than the same volume of water. Discuss icebergs.

(c) *Materials:* a bottle or jar with a cork or a cap, a pan, water, and a food freezer or a refrigerator with a freezing compartment if the outside temperature is above freezing

Fill the bottle or jar with water and close it with the cork or cap. Place the container of water in an empty pan and freeze the water. Take the pan containing the jar or bottle of ice into the classroom and discuss what happens when water freezes and does not have room in its container to expand. Ask what might happen to milk left outside when the weather is cold. Why do water pipes sometimes break in very cold weather?

7. SNOW AND FROST

Materials: an electric hot plate, a pan, a clean white cloth, and snow or frost (from the inside walls of a food freezer if the climate is such that neither snow nor frost occur naturally)

Place some snow or frost in the pan and bring it into the classroom. Either allow the warmth of the room to melt the snow or frost or heat the pan on an electric hot plate. Observe what remains. Strain it through a clean white cloth. Are any foreign particles present? Why will the hands or breath of a person cause snow or frost to melt? If frost is present naturally, discuss why it sparkles in the light.

8. WATER – FORCE

Materials: a glass of water and a sink

Hold your hand over the sink and pour water from the glass onto your hand. Feel it push your hand down. Hold your hand under an open faucet. Notice the force of the water. Discuss water wheels and dams.

Chapter Four

HEAT AND COLD

1. HEAT AND SUNLIGHT

Materials: several small metal articles

Place several metal articles in direct sunlight. If outside temperatures are low, the articles may be placed in the sunlight on a window sill. Place a duplicate set of metal articles in the shade, but close to the other set. Have the children close their eyes and guess by means of touch which articles have been in the sunlight.

2. EVAPORATION

(a) Drying

Materials: two similar pieces of cloth or articles of clothing, water, and two chairs or boxes

Thoroughly wet the pieces of cloth or clothing. Place the wet material over the boxes or chairs. Set one piece to dry in the sunlight and the other to dry in nearby shade. Which piece dries first?

(b) Cooling

Material: water

Moisten one finger and hold it in the wind or blow on it. Note which side becomes cooler. Discuss the fact that evaporation cools. Note that liquids absorb heat when they are vaporized (as in a refrigerator).

3. TEMPERATURE

(a) Weather

Materials: a large calendar or piece of chart paper, a felt pen or crayon, and an outside thermometer

Either secure or construct a calendar large enough to permit daily marking of outside temperatures. Place the thermometer outside and decide what time or times each day you wish to read it and record the temperature. Read the thermometer at the same time or times each day and mark the temperatures on the calendar with the felt pen or crayon. Discuss the variations in temperature. Ask questions such as these: "The weather chart tells us that at 9:30 last Tuesday morning it was 40°; what do you suppose you wore to school that day? Was any day cold (or hot) last week?" Show that such words as cold, colder, hot, warm, etc., are relative, not absolute, terms. Compare temperatures recorded at various times on your chart with temperatures recorded at the same times in other parts of the country.

(b) Heat

Materials: a cooking thermometer, a small kettle or pan, an electric hot plate, and water

Partially fill the kettle or pan with water and place it on the hot plate. Bring the water to a boil and test the temperature with the cooking thermometer. Measure the temperature of tap water. Compare the two and discuss. Use caution when testing boiling water to prevent serious burns!

(c) Thermometer

Materials: a half-pint or one-pint glass bottle, a one-hole rubber stopper (to fit the neck of the bottle), a piece of glass tubing about 1' long (to fit the hole in the stopper), a small amount of red ink or red food coloring, and a felt pen or a grease pencil

Insert the glass tube into the hole in the stopper (not completely through the stopper). Fill the bottle completely with water colored with red ink or red food coloring. Insert the stopper and tube (with the tube pointing up) tightly into the neck of the bottle. Some colored water will be forced into, and will rise in, the glass tube. Mark the top of the red water on the glass tube with a felt pen or a grease pencil. Move the bottle to a warmer place or, if the bottle

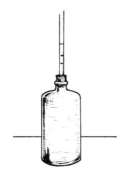

is Pyrex glass, heat it gently on an electric hot plate. Watch the water rise in the tube and, if desired, mark the limit of the rise. You now have a crude thermometer that measures temperature by the expansion of a liquid. (Consideration should also be given to differences produced by atmospheric pressure.)

(d) Taste

Materials: enough whole milk to provide each child participating with one-quarter of a paper cup of milk, a kettle or pot large enough to hold the milk, an electric hot plate, and a paper cup for each child

Pour the milk into the kettle and bring it to a boil on the hot plate. Allow the milk to cool and fill each cup about one-quarter full. Ask the children to taste the milk. Does it taste like milk usually does? Explain that milk is heated to pasteurize it (to kill germs). Why doesn't ordinary pasteurized milk taste like the milk that was heated in the classroom? Explain that milk is pasteurized by heating it to about 145° F. for about 30 minutes rather than by boiling it for a short period. How can the boiling temperature of milk be determined for comparison purposes?

(e) Cold

Materials: two similar containers (such as two one-pound coffee cans) filled with ice cubes or crushed ice, one cup of salt, and two liquid weather thermometers

Place the bulb of one thermometer at least 1″ deep in the untreated ice of one container. Mix the cup of salt with the ice in the second container and place the second thermometer in the mixture in a position similar to the first one. Watch both temperatures fall. Why does the container with ice and salt get colder than the other one? Explain that salt lowers the melting point of ice. The lowest temperature that can be reached by this means is about −9° F. Tell the class how ice cream can be made by using a similar salt and ice mixture to freeze the ice cream mixture. As the ice melts, it takes heat from the ice cream mixture. The ice cream mixture freezes at a lower temperature than does ice, therefore, the ice-salt mixture is needed to provide a lower temperature. Discuss why salting sidewalks and streets will sometimes help to remove ice. Salt lowers the melting point so that the ice will melt even on days when the temperature is below 32° F.

(f) Friction

Materials: a metal button, coin, or other small piece of metal and some woolen cloth

To show that friction produces heat, rub a piece of metal rapidly against the woolen cloth. Note that the metal soon becomes hot. Observe that the harder and faster you rub, the hotter the metal becomes.

(g) Absorption

Materials: a 9" x 12" piece of black paper and paste or masking tape

Tape or paste the black paper on a window pane where it will be in direct sunlight. Feel the paper and the glass next to the paper. Which is warmer? Why do people in some climates wear dark clothing in winter and light colored clothing in summer? Discuss light and dark colored streets, roofs, automobiles, etc.

Chapter Five

AIR

1. RESISTANCE

Materials: two 9" x 12" pieces of note or tablet paper

Wad one piece of paper into a ball and keep the other flat. Drop the two pieces from a height. Note that the air resists the progress of the flat piece more than the wadded one. Make and fly paper airplanes to demonstrate air resistance further.

2. AIR PRESSURE

(a) *Materials:* a metal can with an airtight cover (such as an empty one-pound tobacco or coffee can), a hammer, and a nail

Place the lid on the empty can. Use the hammer and nail to punch one small hole in the top (lid) of the can and one small hole in the bottom of the can. Remove the lid. Hold a finger over the bottom hole and fill the can with water. Replace the lid. Uncover the bottom hole and note that water runs out of the can when both holes are open. Cover the top (lid) hole. Observe and discuss.

(b) *Materials:* a piece of glass tubing 12″ to 18″ long and a container of water

Place a finger over one end of the glass tube. Put the other end of the tube into the container of water. Remove your finger from the top end of the tube and notice that the water rushes into the portion of the tube below the surface of the water. Replace your finger over the top end of the tube and lift the tube above the surface of the water. What happens? Remove your finger from the top end of the tube and again observe what happens. It is possible, with practice, to use this dip tube to pick up bits of material from the bottom of an aquarium. If the amount of time that the top end of the tube is uncovered is watched closely, it is possible to control quite accurately the amount of water that will enter the tube.

(c) *Materials:* a toy rubber balloon, a candle in a holder, matches, and a large container partially filled with water

Blow up the balloon. Feel and press the balloon to note the air pressure inside. Light the candle and blow it out

by letting the air escape from the neck of the balloon. Inflate the balloon again and deflate it under water in the container. Notice the bubbles that escape. This experiment may also be used to illustrate the fact that air occupies space.

3. AIR HAS WEIGHT

Materials: two toy balloons of the same size, a stick of wood or a ruler, string, and a pencil

Fill the two balloons with air until they are about the same size and tie each balloon with a piece of string about 8″ long. Use bow knots for closing the necks of the balloons so that one balloon may later be untied. Tie one balloon to each end of the stick or ruler. Hold the pencil horizontally in your hand and use it as a fulcrum to balance the stick with the balloons. Move the stick to the left or right until a balance is reached. Mark the stick where it crosses the fulcrum (pencil). You now have a crude balance scale. Explain that the weight of the stick and balloon to the left of the mark is about the same as the weight of the stick and balloon to the right of the mark. Remove the stick and balloons from the fulcrum and let the air out of one balloon. Be sure to leave the strings attached to both balloons and to the stick. Now try to balance the stick and balloons with the fulcrum in the same position as before (your mark). Note that one end is heavier than the other. Why is it heavier? Where is the center of balance now?

4. AIR AND FIRE

(a) *Materials:* an asbestos pad, a one-pound coffee can with a lid, a 9″ x 12″ piece of stiff paper, a handfull of dry wood shavings, and two pot holders

Place the can on the asbestos pad and put a small pile of wood shavings in the bottom of the can. Light the shavings to make a small fire. With the stiff paper, fan the fire to show that fanning helps the fire to burn by giving it more "air." Place the lid on the can. Wait a few minutes; then remove the can lid (use pot holders). What happened to the fire? Ask the children what would be likely to happen if a person's clothing caught on fire and he ran. Would the fire burn more rapidly? What would be likely to happen if the person rolled up in a rug or smothered the fire in some other way? Only the teacher should work this experiment.

(b) *Materials:* a dish or saucer, a candle about 3″ long, ink or food coloring, a pint jar, and water

Use some melted wax from the candle to hold it upright in the center of the dish. Color some water with ink or food coloring and pour about ½″ of the water into the dish. Light the candle. Invert the jar and place it over the candle. The edge (lip) of the jar should be resting on the dish. Note that as the fire uses the oxygen in the air inside of the jar, the water goes up in the jar. This experiment helps to show that fire needs "air" to burn. What other concept does it illustrate?

5. AIR MOVEMENT

Materials: two chalkboard erasers, a paper towel, an asbestos pad or another type of fire-resistant pad, and a coffee can

Clap used chalkboard erasers over a radiator or stove. Which way does the dust move? Put a twisted piece of paper towel into the coffee can. Set the can on an asbestos pad and light the paper. Observe the smoke to see air movements. This experiment should be worked only by the teacher.

Chapter Six

MAGNETISM

1. MAGNETS

(a) *Materials:* horseshoe and bar magnets; a tin can; and a variety of such small objects as tacks, bits of paper, feathers, copper pennies, paper clips, and buttons

See which of the small objects the magnets will attract. See if the magnets will attract the tin can. Explain that the can is really mostly sheet iron or steel. Test the magnets with the tacks to see if the magnets are of equal strength over their entire length. Where are they strongest? If an inexpensive magnet is available, break it and test the pieces.

(b) *Materials:* a magnet; a thin piece of paper; pieces of lead, zinc, or wood; a paper clip; string; a nail; thread; a chair; and a thumbtack

To show that magnets attract through various objects, hold a magnet under paper, wood, and other materials. Place a nail on top of the material and observe results. To show that magnets attract through air, place a chair upon a table and hang the magnet by a string from the back rail, about 6″ above the surface of the table. Tack a piece of thread to the table under the magnet. Tie a paper clip to the free end of the thread. The thread should be just long enough so that the paper clip almost touches the magnet. Various objects may be passed through the space

between the clip and magnet to see whether magnetism will pass through the objects in addition to passing through air.

2. MAGNETIC FIELD

Materials: a flat piece of glass or stiff paper, iron filings, and a magnet

Hold the magnet under the paper or glass. Sprinkle iron filings on the paper or glass and observe the field of attraction. Where is the pull strongest?

3. MAKING A MAGNET

Materials: a pocket knife, a needle, steel tacks or iron filings, and a magnet

Make a magnet by taking a piece of hard steel, such as a knife blade, and stroking it in one direction with the end of a magnet. Use the same procedure to magnetize the needle. See if the blade and the needle will attract the tacks or iron filings. Explain that iron may also be magnetized, but that it will not hold its magnetism as long as hard steel.

4. COMPASS

Materials: a needle, a cork, a container of water, nail polish, and a magnet

To make a compass, first magnetize the needle. Then float the cork to determine where to place the needle. The needle should be parallel to the surface of the water. Force the needle halfway through the cork. Float the cork and use the nail polish to mark the end of the needle that points north. Move the ends of the magnet near the ends of the

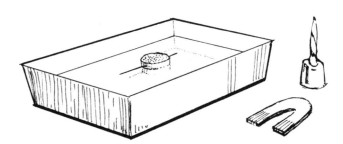

compass needle. What happens? Both the magnet and the needle have north and south poles. Explain that like poles repel and unlike poles attract.

5. HEAT

Materials: a needle, a compass, a magnet, pliers, and a candle in a holder

To show that heat destroys magnetism, first magnetize a needle. Test the needle for magnetism by holding it near the compass. Using pliers, hold the needle over the candle flame until the needle is red hot. Cool the needle and retest it with the compass. Explain that heat softens the steel and causes it to lose its magnetism (although this is but part of the explanation).

Chapter Seven
ELECTRICITY

1. LIGHT

(a) *Materials:* a discarded light bulb, tape, and a desk lamp

Break an old light bulb carefully. Remove all the glass and tape the sharp edges. Examine the interior of the bulb. Note how fine the wires are inside the bulb. Discuss the fact that heat may make light. Observe that this principle is at work in the sun. Use the desk lamp to demonstrate, by feeling the bulb before and after it is lit, that not all the heat is given off as light. Children should not perform this experiment.

(b) *Materials:* one dry cell and a few inches of fine, un-coated, hard wire

Connect the piece of wire to the two poles (terminals) of the dry cell. See the wire get hot and give off light. This experiment soon exhausts a dry cell, so it is better not to prolong this short circuit. Have children rub their hands together to feel the heat from the friction. Discuss the fact that electricity is pushing through the thin wire so fast that it makes much heat. Explain that some metals become white hot from the resistance to the flow of electricity.

2. ELECTRIC SWITCH

Materials: a small block of wood about $\frac{3}{4}''$ x $3''$ x $4''$, a strip of tin about $1''$ x $3''$, two thumbtacks, a hammer, and a nail

To make a simple switch in a wire circuit, first break the complete path of the flow of electricity (circuit) by cutting the wire at the position at which you want to place your switch. Remove the insulation from the last $\frac{1}{2}''$ of each piece of wire (on each side of the cut). Use the hammer and nail to punch a small hole through the tin strip about $\frac{1}{2}''$ from one end. Wrap the stripped end of one wire around the thumbtack. Place the point of the tack through the hole in the tin strip and push the tack into the block about $1''$ from the end of one of the $3''$ x $4''$ sides of the block. The tin strip should be fastened parallel to the length of the block. Wrap the end of the other wire several turns around the second tack. Move the tin aside and push the tack into the block about $1''$ from the other end on the same side where you placed the first tack. The latter tack should now be under the unfastened end of the tin strip. Bend the tin strip so that it is about $\frac{1}{2}''$ away from the tack under it. To operate the switch (close and open), merely push down and release the raised end of the tin strip. This switch should only be used with dry cells. The switch "handle" is not insulated to protect the operator.

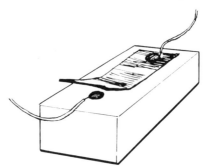

3. ELECTROMAGNET

Materials: an iron bolt about ½" x 4", thin insulated wire, a dry cell, some carpet tacks, and a switch

Wind the insulated wire around the iron bolt. Leave about 1' of wire free before you start winding. Several layers of wire will give more strength. Leave about 1' of wire unwound on the other end. Connect one end of the wire to one terminal post of the dry cell and the other end to the other terminal post. The circuit may be opened and closed by the addition of a switch on one wire between the cell and the bolt. Close the switch and pick up tacks, etc. Open the switch and observe the results. Do not leave the electromagnet connected for long periods.

4. STATIC ELECTRICITY

(a) *Materials:* a carpet, a grounded metal water pipe or radiator, and a piece of manila paper or similar paper about 9" x 12"

Scuff your feet along a carpet and touch a piece of grounded metal (a water pipe, a radiator, etc.). Note the charge of static electricity that "escapes" from your body. Hold the piece of paper between your hands. Rub your feet on the carpet, and "stick" the paper to a wall. Explain the fact that as the paper loses its charge it will drop to the floor. Similar experiments may be made by rubbing toy balloons and "sticking" them to the wall.

(b) *Materials:* a hard rubber or glass rod, a piece of fur or a piece of wool cloth, a comb, and small bits of paper

Rub the rod with the fur or wool. Then note that the rod will pick up tiny pieces of paper. Ask the children if they

have noticed what sometimes happens when they comb dry hair. Use the comb to demonstrate static electricity

5. LIGHT OR BELL CIRCUIT

Materials: a three-volt light bulb and socket, two dry cells, bell wire, a switch, and a bell

Use wire to connect one post of a dry cell to one terminal of the light socket or bell and connect the other post to the other terminal of the light socket or bell. A switch may be wired into the circuit. Connect the dry cell with a second cell to obtain more light from the bulb. Discuss the concept that electricity flows in a "circle." If the "circle" is broken, the flow of electricity stops. Try loosening one wire from a terminal. What happens? Cut one wire and leave a small gap between the wires. Be sure that the switch is closed and try mending the circuit by closing the gap between the wires with various objects, such as scissors, a knife, a penny, a piece of string, paper, glass, etc. Explain that electricity will flow through some materials better than through others. Discuss the difference in strength between the current used in houses (other than in bells and a few other mechanisms) and the current that comes from your dry cells. Children should understand the fire and shock dangers in experimenting with house current.

Chapter Eight

LIGHT AND SOUND

1. LIGHT – MAGNIFIERS

Materials: a magnifying glass, reading glasses, binoculars, a telescope, a small square of flat glass, and a camera

Experiment in the use of the magnifying glass. Compare the appearance of objects seen through the magnifying glass with the appearance of the same objects viewed through ordinary glass. Use the magnifying glass to "gather" sunlight. Feel the heat that is "concentrated." Examine a camera and note the lens. Look at objects through reading glasses, binoculars, and a telescope and discuss.

2. LIGHT–SHADOWS

Material: a desk lamp

Point out that shadows are sometimes long and sometimes short. Mark and measure a shadow cast by the same object in the sunlight in the morning and in the afternoon. Was the shadow in the same place? Can we find out why shadows change? Use the unshaded bulb in the desk lamp to make shadows in the classroom.

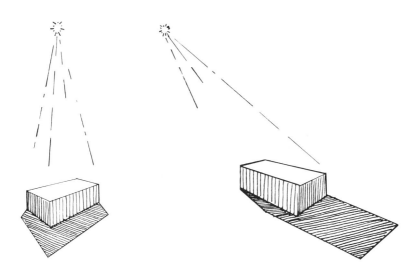

3. LIGHT–COLOR AND REFLECTION

Materials: a glass container, a glass prism, a hand mirror, a magnifying mirror, and water

Observe light through various objects placed in the direct rays of the sun. Look at light that has passed through water in a glass container, through a prism, and through raindrops of water. Reflect light with an ordinary hand mirror and with a magnifying mirror. What happens to the light?

4. SOUND

(a) *Materials:* a bottle, a jar, a barrel, a paper tube, and a tin can

Listen to the sounds made by speaking into a bottle, a jar, a barrel, a paper tube, and a tin can. Try speaking and listening in the auditorium, in the classroom, and outdoors. Compare the sounds heard and discuss. Have the children speak while feeling their throats with their hands.

(b) *Materials:* several similar glass jars or bottles.

Fill several jars or bottles with varying amounts of water. The jars will sound different notes when they are struck. Use a number of different objects for strikers. Do the strikers make a difference in the sound? Why?

(c) *Materials:* a wooden ruler, a triangle (musical instrument), and a tuning fork

Hold a ruler so that part of it extends over the edge of a desk. Bend the end down and then release it and observe the vibration. Experiment with a triangle and a tuning fork. Strike them and touch them lightly to feel the vibrations. Stop the vibrations and note what happens to the sound.

(d) *Material:* a rubber band

Stretch a rubber band from a fixed support, such as the arm of a chair. Pluck the rubber band while tightening and loosening it. Note the changes in vibration and sound. How are the violin, harp, and other string instruments similar in concept to the rubber band of your experiment?

5. SOUND–TIN CAN TELEPHONE

Materials: two clean tin cans (#2 size) with one end smoothly removed from each, two large buttons, about 20′ of string, wax, a hammer, and a nail

Wax the string. Punch a small hole in the center of the remaining end of each can. Thread one end of the string through the hole in one can (from the outside to the inside) and tie this end of the string to a button. Fasten the other can and button to the other end of the string in the same

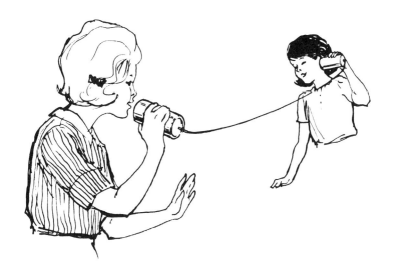

manner. Stretch the string tightly by moving the cans apart. Have one child speak quietly directly into one can while a second child holds the other can to his ear to listen. Compare speaking and listening with and without the aid of the "telephone."

6. SOUND – SPOON CHIME

Materials: a spoon and a piece of string about 36″ long

Make a spoon chime by tying the spoon in the middle of the string. Wrap one end of the string once or twice around the left index finger and the other around the right index finger. Put one finger in each ear, leaving the spoon to dangle supported only by the string. Swing the spoon against a table edge. Does the person with the string in his ears hear the sound better than the others? Why?

7. SOUND – DRUMS

Materials: round cheese, oatmeal, or ice cream boxes; a tin can with top and bottom removed; inner tube rubber; and cord

Use the boxes as drums. Make a tom-tom by stretching inner tube rubber over the open ends of a tin can. Secure the rubber with cord. Try various strikers. Why does a drum make its own peculiar sound?

Chapter Nine

MOVING THINGS

1. FRICTION

(a) On the surface

Materials: a block of wood, a brick, a book, thread, and
string

Try pulling such objects as a block of wood, a brick, and
a book over various rough and smooth surfaces. Use a
piece of string to pull the objects. Then try pulling the
objects with a length of thread. Why does the thread sometimes break when the object is pulled on some surfaces?

(b) In the air

Materials: two similar 9″ x 12″ sheets of paper

Wad one sheet of paper loosely into a ball the size of a
baseball or larger. Crumple the other sheet into a ball the
size of a golf ball or smaller. Throw both pieces of wadded
paper through the air. Do both pieces have the same
weight? Why does the smaller ball pass through the air
more easily?

(c) In water

Materials: a container of water, a tennis ball with a rough
exterior, and a rubber ball of about the same
size and weight as the tennis ball and with a
smooth exterior

Twirl the tennis ball in water. Twirl the rubber ball in
water. Which ball twirls more easily? Which spins longer?

2. REDUCING FRICTION

Materials: a flat piece of glass or wood about 1′ x 2′, half
of a common brick, oil, soap, water, and several
books

Make a gradual incline on a table by raising one end of the
piece of glass and supporting it in this position by a few

books. Try sliding the piece of brick down the dry glass. Wet the glass and try sliding the brick. Rub soap on the glass and try again. What happens? Cover a portion of the surface with oil and again try sliding the piece of brick. For discussion purposes, compare this experiment with the situations involved with auto tires and mud, shoes and a wet floor, etc.

3. USES OF FRICTION

Materials: a jar or Thermos bottle with a cover, soap, and water

Do we always want to get rid of friction? Try removing a fairly tight cover from a jar or Thermos bottle with dry hands and with soapy hands. Why must we be careful of water on a floor? Why do accidents sometimes happen when people are in bathtubs? Explain that friction is often used to "hold" things. Discuss walking, using auto or bicycle brakes, etc.

4. WHEELS AND ROLLERS

Materials: a round oatmeal box cover, cardboard, a pencil, a coffee can lid, and about a dozen marbles

Punch a hole through the middle of the box cover and push the pencil halfway through the hole. Explain that you now have a wheel and axle. Cut out various shapes and sizes of wheels from a piece of cardboard. Punch holes through the centers, add axles, and try rolling the wheels. Do some roll more easily than others? Place a coffee can cover over about a dozen marbles grouped on a table. Place a book or other heavy object on the cover. Spin the object and the cover. Remove the marbles and try to spin the object. Discuss the results.

5. LEVERS

Materials: a ruler, a pencil, a flat rock or piece of.brick 3" or 4" square, 8' or 10' of 2" x 10" or 12" board, and several bricks

To demonstrate the use of levers for lifting, lay the ruler across the pencil (fulcrum). Place a flat rock or piece of brick on the end of the ruler that is resting on the table. Try pressing on the other end of the ruler to lift the rock.

Place the pencil, or fulcrum, at different places under the ruler. Does this make a difference in lifting the object? Is greater pressure needed when the fulcrum is near the raised end? Is the object raised the same distance each time? Center the board over several bricks stacked two bricks high. Try to balance a "heavy" and a "light" child on the ends of the board. Use other children to steady the children on the board. Move the board on the bricks (fulcrum) and again try to balance the two children. Adjust the board and fulcrum until the two children are balanced. Note the lengths of the plank from the fulcrum to the ends and discuss.

6. INCLINED PLANE

(a) *Materials:* a rubber band, a roller skate, and a flat board about 1' by 3' long

Attach the rubber band to the roller skate. Grasp the end of the rubber band and pull the skate straight up. Note the stretch in the rubber band. Use the board and stack of books to make a slanted surface, or inclined plane, as in Experiment 2. Try pulling the skate with the rubber band several times with the board held at different slants (pitch). Note that the rubber band stretches more as the pitch increases.

(b) *Materials:* assorted bolts and screws

State that bolts and screws contain inclined planes. Closely examine several bolts and screws. Observe that the threads gradually move from one end to the other. What would happen if the "spiral" of the threads moved very quickly on the screw or bolt? Does the experiment with the skate tell us what to expect?

7. SIMPLE MACHINES

(a) Drawbridge

Materials: a ¾" x 6" x 24" board, a ¾" x 6" x 12" board, four ¾" x 2" x 12" pieces of wood, four small pulleys, two pieces of leather 1" square, nails, tacks, counterweights, and string

Use the 6" x 24" board for a base (roadway). Join the 6" ends of the 6" x 12" piece and the 6" x 24" piece with leather hinges. (Lay the pieces end to end and place the leather hinges across the joint about ½" from each outside edge. Use tacks to fasten the hinges to each piece.) You now have the lift portion attached to the base. To attach the pulley towers, nail one 2" x 12" piece of wood to each side of the base. The 12" pieces should be fastened in a vertical position to the sides of the base right next to the hinged joint. Attach a small pulley to the side or top of each tower. Fasten a string to each unhinged corner of the bridge (portion that lifts); run the string through the pulleys and try out different counterweights on the ends of the strings. Discuss weights—their sizes, weights, and uses. Select weights that balance the weight of the draw-bridge lift. Build approaches to each side of the bridge and operate the bridge. Other types of drawbridges may be built. Towers may be placed on both ends and the whole center portion raised by means of four pulleys and weights.

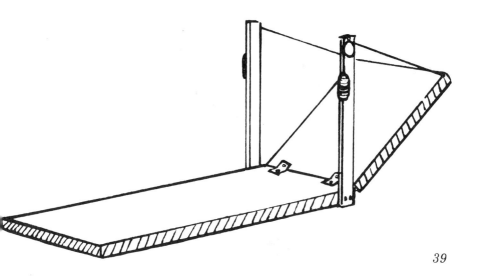

(b) Elevator

Materials: one orange crate without a center partition, a cardboard box about 10″ x 10″ x 12″ deep, two pulleys, cord, two screw hooks, a stapler and staples, and counterweights

Stand the crate (elevator shaft) on end and attach each pulley with a screw hook near the top of the inside of the shaft at the midpoint of the side. Place the cardboard box inside the shaft with the open part of the box facing the same way as the open front of the shaft. Staple a piece of cord roughly one and a half times the length of the shaft to the midpoint of each side of the cage (box) near the top. Run the cords through the pulleys and attach counterweights. If desired, four pulleys may be used by attaching a cord to each corner of the top of the cage and placing the pulleys in each corner at the top of the shaft. Holes may be drilled through the sides of the shaft near the top and the pulleys and weights placed on the outside of the shaft. A buzzer or bell system may also be installed. (See Experiment 5, Chapter Seven.)

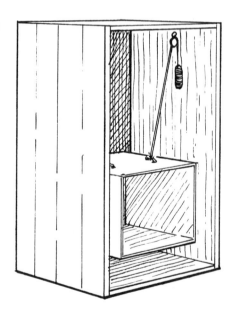